**MAKE
YOUR OWN
ANIMATED
MOVIES**

MAKE YOUR OWN ANIMATED MOVIES

Yellow Ball Workshop Film Techniques

by Yvonne Andersen

Little, Brown and Company
BOSTON   TORONTO

LIBRARY OF CONGRESS CATALOG CARD NO. 74-117025

Second Printing

Published simultaneously in Canada
by Little, Brown & Company (Canada) Limited

PRINTED IN THE UNITED STATES OF AMERICA

ACKNOWLEDGMENTS

Dominic Falcone, my husband,
and our children, Jean and Paul Falcone

My film students at the Yellow Ball Workshop, Cellar Door
Cinema, Project Inc., and the Newton Creative Arts Center

My assistants at these schools: Dominic Falcone, Marjorie Lenk,
Mary Austin, Joanne Ricca, Elizabeth Archer, and Carol Sones

And also
Marjorie Lenk, director, Cellar Door Cinema; Albert Hurwitz,
coordinator of the arts, Newton Public Schools; Rita DeLisi,
former director, Project Inc.; Rev. John Culkin, S.J., director,
Center for Understanding Media; Anthony Hodgkinson,
assistant professor of film, Department of Public Communication,
Boston University; Gerald O'Grady, director, Media Center,
University of St. Thomas, Houston, Texas; Harris Cohen and
staff, Back Bay Film Lab, Boston, Massachusetts; The
Dephoures, D-4 Film Studio Inc., Newton Corner, Massachusetts;
Bernt Pettersen, president, Envision Corporation, Boston,
Massachusetts; Alvin Fiering, president, Polymorph Films Inc.,
Boston, Massachusetts.

CONTENTS

**MAKE
YOUR OWN
ANIMATED
MOVIES**

MAKING FILMS
AT THE YELLOW BALL WORKSHOP

The Yellow Ball Workshop in Lexington, Massachusetts, is a place where children and adults make animated films. The students in our classes do their own art, story, animation, camera work, editing and sound. The animation techniques developed at the workshop have been taught at other schools and in educational systems throughout the country. Since 1963, when the workshop first opened, we have worked to develop techniques to help the individual young person make films in the simplest and most expressive way.

The art supplies we use are those easily obtained by anyone. Although we use mostly 16 mm film equipment in our classes, our students have also made animated films using their own inexpensive 8 mm and Super-8 mm equipment.

Film animation is an important new form of artistic expression. It combines the graphic arts of painting, drawing and sculpture with the art and techniques of theatre and film. The animated film is most often associated with humor, but it can also be used to express joy, terror, pathos, tenderness and social comment. Our students are encouraged to consider it first as a means of making their paintings and drawings come magically to life.

To achieve this, the film animator needs only his own artwork and some basic film equipment. He need not have actors, scenery, technical crews, makeup, or any of the cumbersome and expensive things needed in live-action filming. He can sit down in a room all by himself and draw his actors and their scenes on small pieces of paper. Then, through his own efforts, he can make them come to life on the screen.

A large part of our work at the Yellow Ball Workshop has been with people between the ages of five and eighteen. This has been exciting. We have had fun, and we have found our students to be serious, hard-working artists who have important contributions to make. People of this age have special qualities. They can work directly and simply without too much premeditation.

Because they are "new people," they can see things in a new way, making interesting and important social comments and inventing marvelous new techniques in which to work. The classes have been a constant adventure. Some of the ways we make films are described in this book. They include cutouts, flip cards, three-dimensional puppet animation, clay animation, drawing on film, pixillation and collage. Our films have been shown in museums, libraries, and schools, and on national television; they have won many awards in international film festivals.

The Yellow Ball Workshop began as a Saturday art class. As one of our projects, I had let the class use my camera equipment to make some short experiments in animation. One Saturday a twelve-year-old student, Steve DeTore, asked if we could make a science fiction film. I said we could if he would prepare the script. The next week he arrived with the story for *The Amazing Colossal Man* . . .

the Amazing Colossal Man

Strange stars and planets drift in space. There is a burst of smoke from the planet Aros, and a silver rocket leaps with a roar into the sky. Its exhaust spells out "The Amazing Colossal Man." The space ship lands on Earth, and a crowd of curious earthlings gathers around the strange object. Suddenly, the door opens and the creature from Aros appears. He is huge and frightening. The earth people scream and fall over each other in their attempt to escape. The creature follows them. He presses between buildings, his huge size causing them to collapse. A woman faints. The earthlings call an emergency meeting.

A professor draws a picture of the creature on a blackboard. "He is fifty feet high, and the only way we can defeat him is by atomic weapons," he says. The general, saluting, agrees. Meanwhile the creature clumps down a tree-lined road with the army in pursuit. Soldiers creep up on the monster from the top of a roller coaster and shoot at him. The creature grabs one in his fist and dashes him to the ground. The hospital corps carry off the injured soldier. A tank gun kills the creature.

Back on Aros, all this has been observed by the Aros scientist with his magic telescope. He says, "Oh no, it couldn't be!" Quickly he presses buttons and turns knobs. There is a buzzing sound. The earthlings look in the sky and see a vast horde of Aros ships heading toward Earth. Their exhausts spell out "The End."

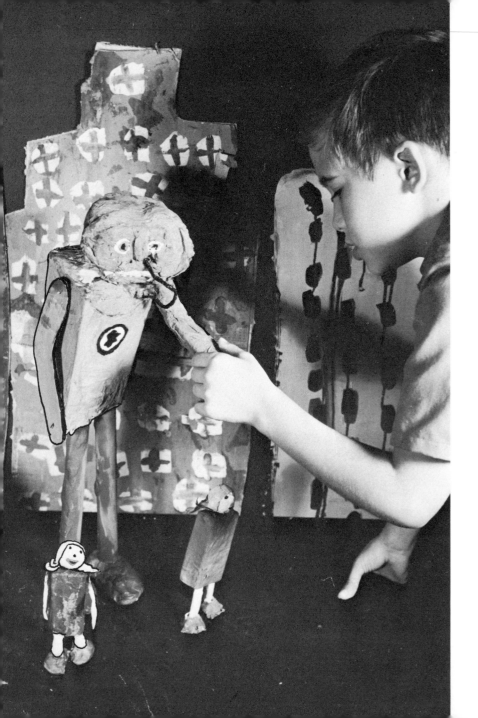

The Amazing Colossal Man was the first animated film created by the students at the Yellow Ball Workshop, in the 1963-1964 session. Twelve students five to twelve years old worked on the film, creating the art, story, camera work, animation, and editing and sound. Steve DeTore, aged twelve, wrote the script. The creature was made by Arthur DeTore, aged ten. The set was propped up on a large table in a room with many windows. No extra lighting was used. The film in the camera was Kodachrome II. All filming was done by daylight.

6

The characters were made using small cardboard boxes, wooden dowels, clay, large nails and papier-mâché. The body was a cardboard box covered with papier-mâché. The bottom was left open for the legs. The head was a ball of clay wrapped around a large nail and covered with papier-mâché. The lower part of the nail formed the neck. The arms were cut out of corrugated cardboard. A nail was pushed through each shoulder and the cardboard arm was then covered with papier-mâché. The legs were long, round wooden dowels, with lumps of clay stuck on the bottom for feet. The legs and feet were covered with papier-mâché, leaving the bottom of each foot uncovered.

When the papier-mâché was dry, the parts were painted with poster paint. A large lump of clay was pushed into the upper part of the box. The nail with the head on the end of it was stuck down into the clay. The clay held the head on and allowed it to be turned from side to side. Next, the nails with the arms on them were pushed into the box at the shoulder positions. They also moved and would hold their position. Then the long wooden dowels which formed the legs were pushed up through the opening at the bottom of the box and into the clay. The small amount of clay left exposed on the bottom of the feet helped the character stick to the ground and hold its position.

7

The sets and large props were also made from cardboard boxes. Dramatic impact was provided by the cameraman, who varied the angle and distance of the shots in each scene. For example, when the rocket ship lands, there is a long shot showing the people running around. The shot when the door opens is a close-up, featuring the face of the monster. Next comes a long shot showing the people running down the street, with the creature following them. The woman fainting is a medium shot which shows her and the sidewalk she falls on.

At times, these papier-mâché characters must talk. Their regular mouths have been painted on very small. Larger cutout mouths are laid on top for the talking scenes.

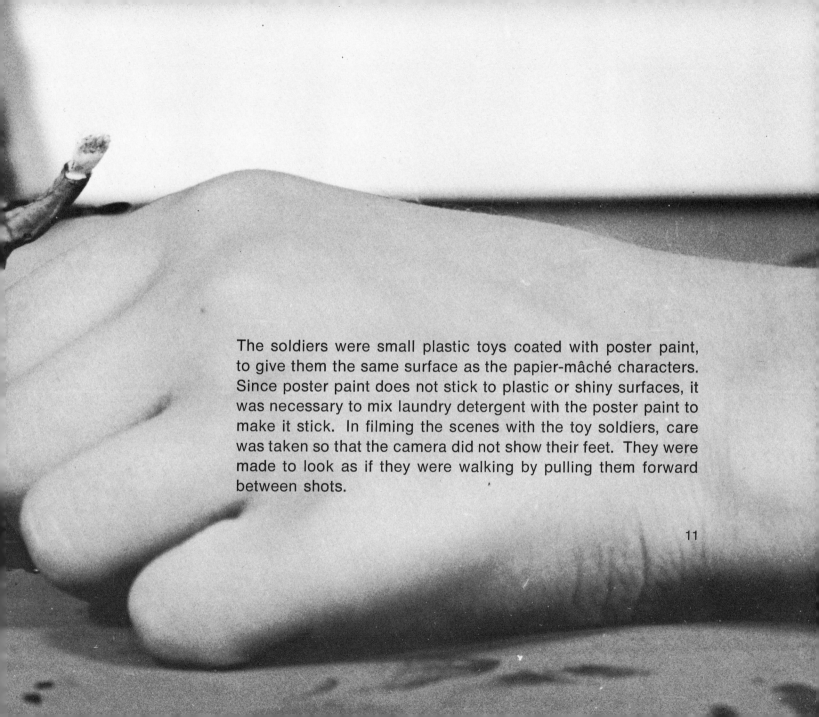

The soldiers were small plastic toys coated with poster paint, to give them the same surface as the papier-mâché characters. Since poster paint does not stick to plastic or shiny surfaces, it was necessary to mix laundry detergent with the poster paint to make it stick. In filming the scenes with the toy soldiers, care was taken so that the camera did not show their feet. They were made to look as if they were walking by pulling them forward between shots.

CUTOUTS

A ship floats on a green ocean. Suddenly, a huge sea serpent rises from the waves and swallows the ship. This is a scene from *Underwater Creatures.* Everything in it was made out of paper. The serpent, ship, and waves were painted and then cut out. The action in the film was created by moving these cutouts around on top of the painted background.

Cutouts are one of the easiest animation techniques. The artwork is put flat on a low table. The movie camera, on a tripod, is pointed down at it. The camera operator presses the single-frame button to take a few pictures (frames). He moves the paper character slightly. Then he takes a few more frames. When this film is run through a projector, the paper character will seem to move all by himself.

Faces

In cutout animation, the first scene to paint is the face of your main character. This portrait should be large, filling most of the page. Any parts which will have to move should not be painted in. If the mouth is to move, paint three different-sized mouths on a separate piece of paper and cut them out. There should be a small mouth in closed position, a slightly bigger mouth partly open and a large mouth wide open. These different mouths will be laid onto the face and filmed in alternation. The face will then be able to talk, whisper, yawn, eat, or smoke.

In this scene from *$50,000 per Fang,* two soldiers stand at the gate of a ruined castle. One says: "Creepy-looking joint, ain't it?" The other answers: "Yeah, we're supposed to meet the guard here." The only movements in the scene are those of the soldiers' mouths.

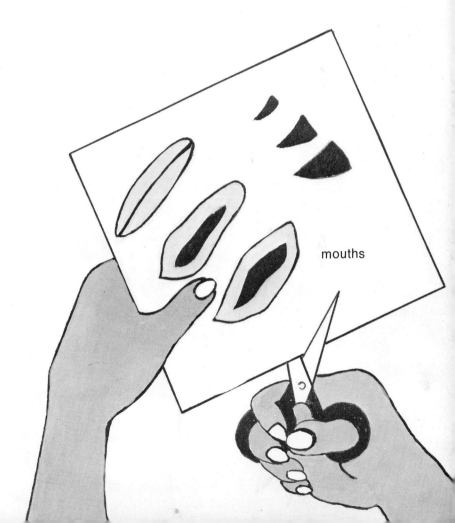

mouths

Other examples of face animation are shown here. In this scene from *In The Middle,* the girl says, "Hi!" In the film, the word seems to puff out of her mouth and then disappear. This is done by making three different-sized balloons: small, medium and large. The girl is first filmed for 24 frames (pictures) with no balloon. Then she is filmed for about 4 frames with the small balloon. Then the small balloon is removed and the medium one laid in its place.

The medium balloon is filmed for 4 frames. It is removed and replaced with the large balloon. This is filmed for about 8 frames. The large balloon is removed and replaced with the medium one, which is filmed for 4 frames. Then the small one is filmed for 4 frames. Finally the girl is filmed for 24 frames with no action. This entire scene lasts for three seconds, or 72 frames.

16

In *Al Kaseltzer Strikes Again,* the gangster reaches into the scene with his hand and lights a cigarette with a burning match. He blows out the match. Smoke floats up from the cigarette, which is burning shorter. The gangster wiggles his eyebrows, looks from one side to the other, blinks, and says, "They will probably have a double guard at the bank!"

This scene is longer and more complex. More things happen. The arm, which is a cutout, must be moved slowly upward into the scene, one-quarter inch for every 2 frames taken. The match flame burns continually. The flickering effect of fire is made by changing the flame every 2 frames. The end of the cigarette is painted red when it is lit, and is cut shorter and shorter during filming. Other movements are those of the eyes, eyebrows, and smoke.

17

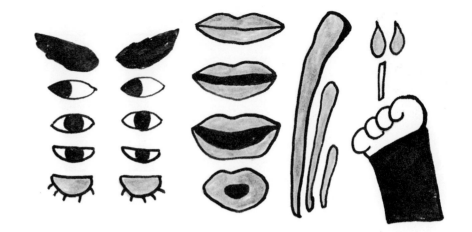

Figures

The next step in your film is to create the body of your character. You have already made his face. Now paint his face again, very much smaller, and connected to a body with hinged arms and legs. Most of the time you will be filming a picture area about 14 inches wide and 11 inches high. The character will move about in that area. He should not be taller than 7 inches if he is to be against a background 11 inches high. If he is to face front, the head, body and legs can be painted together. The arms should be painted separately, slightly bent at the elbows. When the character is cut out, the arms can be hinged onto the body with pieces of masking tape pasted on the reverse side.

For more flexible arm movements, use thread with the masking tape. Tape a piece of thread to the back of the top part of the arm. Tape the other end of the thread to the back of the shoulder. If the two pieces of tape are close together, the joint will be firm.

You don't have to fasten the arms and legs to the body at all: you can work with them loose. But there are disadvantages to this method. If the character is accidentally jolted, the arms and legs may fly in all directions, and you may not get them back in the right place again. And if the character must be used again later, you may find that an arm or leg is lost, and must be remade.

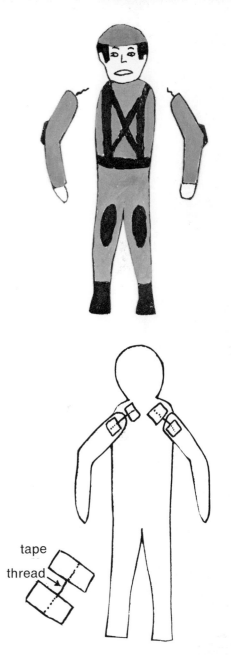

tape

thread

19

If a character is to walk across a scene, he should be drawn sideways and his legs should be hinged. He will have a more natural movement if his arms are hinged as well. His head and body are made in one piece. The tops of the legs are hinged to the lower part of the body with tape and thread. The legs should be painted slightly bent, to give them a more natural look when he walks. The legs and the arms may also be hinged at the elbows and the knee, but this is not necessary in most cases, and it is much harder.

Backgrounds

What are the character's surroundings, or background? Where is he? Is he at home, in a public building, in the city, the forest, on the ocean? What will he do? What might happen to him? In this scene from *$50,000 per Fang,* the soldier is walking through a swamp forest. The top trees are cutouts, laid on top of a painted forest. The soldier can be made to walk either in front or in back of the trees. This gives the forest a three-dimensional look and helps to create atmosphere. The soldier is on his way to the castle of vampires. On the following pages are examples of other types of backgrounds for cutouts.

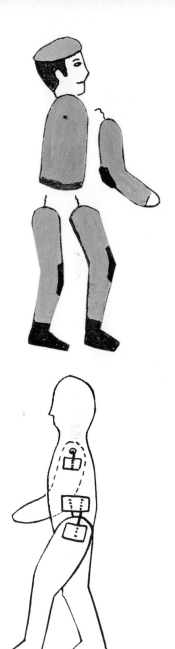

Backgrounds can be simple or complex. This background for *Stanley the Pink Unicorn* is a simple one. It has a blue sky, white snow, and brown tree stumps. The tree stumps are cutouts taped on top of the snow. In this scene, Stanley chops wood with his teeth to build a fire so that his friends can keep warm.

In this scene from *Cinder City* the background is a city waterfront at night. The only thing that moves is a red ship, which bobs slightly on the waves. The sound effects are foghorn, water lapping, and ropes creaking. The background is painted on a sheet of paper. The ship is a cutout.

22

Blue sky, gray mountains and red-brown earth are the background for *Atomic Robot*. This setting is used several times in the film. It is first used when the spaceship lands and blasts a hole in the earth, and then again when the spaceship takes off from behind the mountains. It also provides background when the Atomic Robot appears and beams a light ray from his head.

Real junk was used in this junkyard scene from *Sylvia I*. The filmmakers ransacked several trash baskets to find old candy wrappers, labels from tin cans, cigarette butts and tinfoil. Later in the film, the characters construct a spaceship from the contents of the junkyard. The spaceship was powered with blinking Christmas-tree lights.

23

Titles

Titles are important. They start and end the film. The beginning title carries the name of the film and the name of the filmmaker. The end of the film is shown with the words "The End," or "End," or "Stop." When a film starts with a good title, it sets the tone for the rest of the film. If the title is sloppy, the audience may assume that the rest of the film will be sloppy too.

The lettering should be simple, bold, very readable and well positioned on the page. You can paint the title on a sheet of colored paper. On a different paper you can paint your name. Another method is to paint the letters and cut them out. This way you can experiment with positioning the letters and even animating them.

It is always more interesting to try to integrate the title with the rest of the film. This can be done by using cutout letters and one of the characters from the film. In *Stanley the Pink Unicorn,* Stanley gallops out onto a black background. The title letters move out after him. He gallops out again, and the name of the filmmaker follows him.

The end title may also be integrated. In *The Mailman and the Dog,* a group of dogs chase a postman, who jumps into a pool of water. The dogs all stand around waiting as "The End" appears on the surface of the water in bubbles. In *Three Blind Mice,* the red, blue, and green mice escape from the farmer's wife into a mousehole. They pull the doors shut after them. On the back of the doors are the words "The End."

The MailMan And the Dog
BY RITA Fantasia And Janet YATES
BEware of DOG
U.S
MAIL U.S.
BEWARE OF DOG

Storyboards

A storyboard is a rough sketch of the different scenes in the film. A page of paper is divided into squares. Each square contains a rough cartoon of the action. In the first square, you may have the title of the film. The next square will have your name. The third square will have your first scene sketched out. Each square represents a scene from the film. Underneath each square you may have a one-line description of the action.

Some people like to make a complete storyboard first. Others prefer to make a storyboard later just to check the organization of the film. On the left are the actual scenes from *The Mailman and the Dog*.

Special Effects

Atmospheric effects look great on the screen. Snow can be made in different ways. In this scene from *Spectator,* the snow-flakes were separate cutouts. Each time the camera operator took 2 frames, each flake was moved downward about one-quarter inch. One person animated the snow, another the man, and another operated the camera. This same technique can be used for rain.

The double exposure is an easier technique for snow or rain. First the scene is filmed without snow, with the lens diaphragm closed down ½ stop to decrease the light. For example, if the opening is supposed to be 8, it is changed to a spot between 8 and 11. A careful record is kept of the footage count. If the scene was started at twenty-five feet and animated for a distance of three feet, this information is written down.

Then the lens cover is put over the lens. The film is rewound in the camera back to the spot where the filming started — at 25 feet. The snow portion is filmed on top of the first portion, again with the light closed down ½ stop. The snow is painted on a long black scroll. The bottom of the scroll is placed under the camera. Every 2 frames, the entire scroll is moved down one-quarter inch. This technique saves the trouble of moving each flake of snow. But to use it, you must have a camera which can be rewound.

Underwater effects may be created in several ways. One way is to film the scene through water. Position a large, clear, flat-bottomed dish of water between the camera and the art. This dish can be held by an assistant, or kept in position by a temporary support. The water should be jiggled slightly between each filming. This will distort the artwork below, causing it to wiggle back and forth as if it were underwater.

The scene opposite from *Yellow Submarine* was done by using three painted blue backgrounds. The brush stroke on each background was different. On top of the blue background was laid a sheet of glass. The submarine and other cutouts were animated on top of the glass. Every 2 frames of filming, the sheet of blue paper was pulled out and a new one put in its place. This produced a shimmering, quivering water background.

You must be careful of one thing when using this technique. A picture of the camera and the filmmaker will be reflected from the glass surface back up into the camera lens. You can avoid this reflection by attaching a black shield around the camera. Cut a small circle in the middle of a sheet of black cardboard. The circle should be just large enough for the lens of the camera to fit through. The cardboard is held onto the lens by a small adapter ring which is screwed onto the front of the lens.

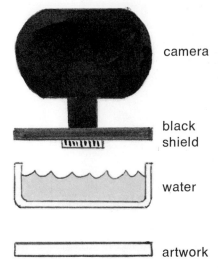

camera

black
shield

water

artwork

Pans

Pictured on the preceding page is the first scene from *Charlie and His Harley,* a motorcycle film by Mark Mahoney, aged twelve. In a pan, the camera starts on the left and seems to move slowly across the faces of the gang as they speak and blink their eyes. The first face blinks his eyes, the second man moves his mouth to say in an outraged tone, "If that guy ain't here in ten minutes, he ain't going to join this club!" The third guy mumbles, "Ah, shet up." The fourth says, "He's got a nice bike."

Although the camera seems to move across the group, creating the feeling of a crowd, in reality the camera is still and the artwork is moved under the camera. Two narrow strips of wood are tacked down to the top of the filming table to form a groove through which the long narrow artwork can be slid. The camera only shows part of the picture at one time. The first part is filmed for about 24 frames, so the audience will get used to seeing the scene. Then the animator slides the artwork to the left about one-eighth of an inch. The cameraman takes 2 frames, the artwork is slid to the left another one-eighth inch, and the camera takes another 2 frames. This continues until the whole scene has been filmed. At the end, 24 frames are taken. As the art is moved, the mouth is animated for whichever character is under the camera.

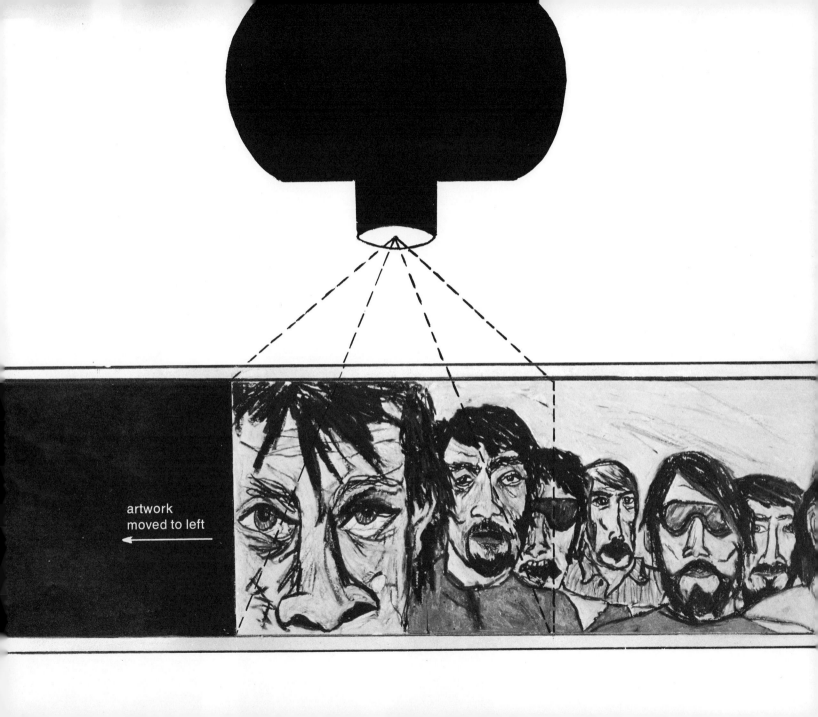

artwork
moved to left

Fades

Movies often begin with a fade-in. This means that the scene starts dark and gradually gets lighter until it is properly lit. This is a smooth and gradual way of starting. This page shows the fade-in made in 6 frames, but it is usually made in 12 or more frames. There are different ways to make a fade. Our method is to start filming the scene with the diaphragm closed. Every 2 frames of filming, we open the lens diaphragm ¼ stop, until we reach the proper stop.

36

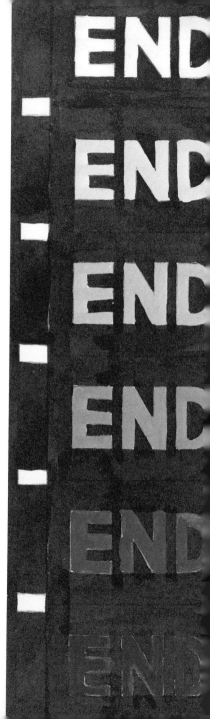

fade-out is used at the end of
 film. Here, END gets darker
d darker until total darkness
 reached. For this, we close
wn the diaphragm ¼ stop ev-
y 2 frames of filming.

issolves

 dissolve is a combination of fade-out and fade-in. The first
ene slowly fades out, while the second scene is fading in
derneath. At the middle point of a dissolve, you can see both
enes in a double exposure. Your camera must have a back-
nd in order to do this. First film a fade-out, counting the
mber of frames it takes. Then cover the lens, disengage the
ars of the camera, and wind the film back to the place where
u started. Then place the new artwork under the lens and film
ade-in. You will then have a dissolve. On this page, a smiling
ce dissolves into END.

SETTING UP THE CAMERA

THE MOVIE CAMERA can be 8 mm, Super-8 mm or 16 mm. It should have reflex viewing and reflex focusing, and a single framing device. If you are buying new equipment, inform the camera store that you will be filming artwork which will be about 18 inches away from the camera. If your present camera does not have these three devices, you can solve the problem with a little work, as described on the next few pages.

THE TRIPOD holds the camera firmly, pointed down at the artwork on the table. It is important that neither the table nor the tripod move during animation. The two front legs of the tripod are braced against the front of the table.

THE TABLE is a small, low one, to hold the artwork during filming. If the table is rickety, it should be firmly braced against a wall or a heavy piece of furniture.

THE LIGHT STANDS are placed on either side of the table, pointed down at the artwork at a 45-degree angle. They are used if you are filming in a dark room using indoor film. If you work near a window which always gives good light, you can use outdoor film in your camera and you won't need light stands.

THE LIGHT METER is pointed at the artwork to see how much light is available for filming. If your camera has an electric eye, you won't need a light meter.

Single Framing

A strip of movie film is a series of separate pictures (frames) in vertical position. In sound movies these run through the projector at the rate of 24 frames per second (f.p.s). Each frame shows a picture just slightly different from the one before it. In live action filming, the button is pressed on the camera, and 24 frames are taken every second the button is held down. A camera with a single framing device allows the cameraman to take just 1 frame each time the button is pressed. He then moves the artwork slightly and takes another frame. When these separate frames are later run through the projector, at the rate of 24 each second, the animated character will seem to move by himself.

In most of our animation, we take 2 frames at a time. If your camera does not have single framing, try just tapping the release button each time, in an effort to take as few frames as possible. You can get an animated effect if the camera takes 4 or even 8 frames between each movement. If your camera can be set to a speed of 8 or 12 f.p.s., you will then have an even better chance of controlling the number of frames taken.

40

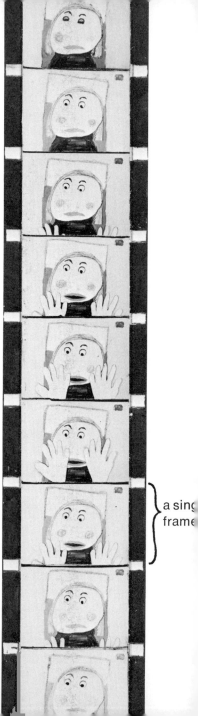

a single frame

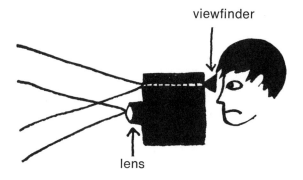

viewfinder

lens

camera without reflex viewing
has a parallax problem

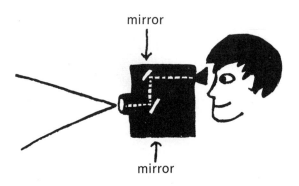

mirror

mirror

camera with reflex viewfinder
films exactly what the eye sees

Reflex Viewing

Reflex viewing means that when you look through the viewfinder, you see exactly what the camera lens is taking. This is done with a system of mirrors something like those in a periscope. On some cameras without reflex viewing, the viewfinder is on the top right side of the camera, and the actual lens taking the picture is on the lower left side.

This does not make much difference in live action filming, where the subject is a great distance from the camera. In animation, where the artwork may be about 18 inches from the camera, it causes a problem called parallax. What you see through the viewfinder is not exactly what the camera lens is taking. You may find that you have filmed half the art and half the table.

If the camera does not have reflex viewing, you must be sure that the actual taking lens of the camera is centered over the artwork, no matter what you see through the viewfinder. Our method is to slip a long cardboard tube over the camera lens. Mark the center of the artwork. Lower the camera until the tube is directly over the center. Remove the tube.

The lens will now take a centered picture. It is a good idea to place your artwork on a black surface, in case the camera takes a little more on all sides than you expect. Even if your camera has reflex viewing, it may take about three-quarters of an inch more all around than you can see through the viewfinder. If these overlapping edges are black, they will not show up when the film is projected in a dark room.

cardboard tube is slipped around lens to center artwork

tube is removed and artwork is ready to film

Reflex Focusing

There are some cameras which have reflex viewing, but not reflex focusing. Reflex focusing means that you can focus your subject sharply by looking through the viewfinder and twisting the distance ring on the lens. You can actually see if you are in focus or not.

Some cameras with reflex focusing cannot focus on anything closer to the camera than 4 feet. This problem can be solved by purchasing a small close-up lens and an adapter ring to hold it onto the camera lens. You can now focus on close objects by looking through the viewfinder and twisting the distance ring until the artwork looks sharp and clear.

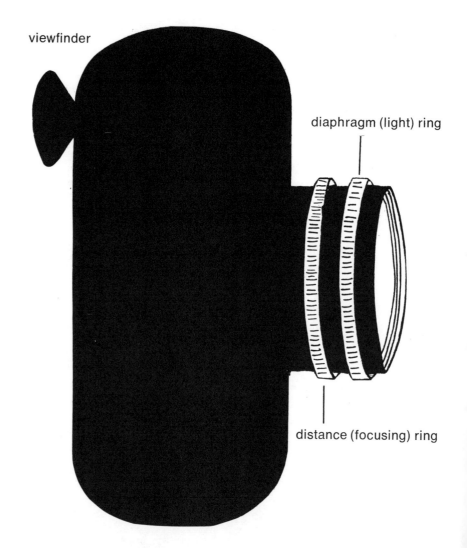

viewfinder

diaphragm (light) ring

distance (focusing) ring

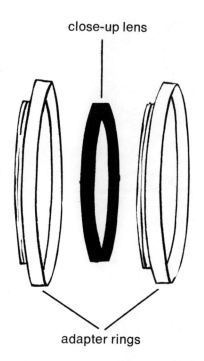

close-up lens

adapter rings

If your camera does not have reflex focusing at all, and the directions tell you to set the distance ring for various footages when you are filming, you can still buy a close-up lens. You must buy the specific ones described in the instruction booklet which comes with the camera. The booklet will also give detailed directions about how far away the camera must be from the art-work when a certain lens is used. The measurement is always made from the film plane to the subject.

If you are using an old camera and cannot find an instruction booklet, bring the camera to the store and buy a close-up lens to fit. On your first roll of film, start with the artwork 8 inches away from the camera. Take about three feet of film. Move the camera back 9 inches away from the artwork. Take three feet of film. Continue doing this until the camera is about 24 inches away from the artwork. Keep a careful record of what you have done. When the film comes back from processing, examine it to see which distance from the artwork gave you the sharpest picture. From then on, always keep the camera that far away when doing animation.

Exposure

If you go outside on a bright snowy day, your eyes will squint shut to keep out the extra light. In a dark room, your eyes will open wide to see clearly. The diaphragm ring on a camera behaves the same way. If there is too much light it closes down. If there is not enough light it opens up. The diaphragm ring opens and closes automatically only if your camera has an electric eye.

If there is no electric eye, you will have to open and close the diaphragm by hand. There are markings on the ring. They start at 1.6, which is a wide-open diaphragm, used when there is not much light. The openings then decrease to 2, 2.8, 4, 5.6, 8, 11, 16, and 22. Twenty-two is a nearly closed diaphragm. This is used when there is too much light. When using a camera without an electric eye, you will need a separate light meter. The light meter is held in the hand and pointed at the artwork. It will tell you if there is enough light on the artwork, and where the diaphragm ring should be set. There are many different kinds of light meters. We like the inexpensive ones which have the movie markings clearly indicated.

diaphragm ring

diaphragm open at 1.6

diaphragm almost closed at 22

These are the steps to take if your camera does not have an electric eye:

1   Load the film into the camera. Inside the box of film will be directions for its use, including its ASA rating. This is its light sensitivity. If the ASA is 25, set the ASA dial of the light meter to 25.

2   Check to see which camera speed you are using. There may be a dial on the side of your camera to set this. In 16 mm animation, we normally use a camera setting of 16 f.p.s.

3   Read the directions which came with your light meter. If you have one of the types with movie markings, point the meter at the artwork and line up the two pointers. Whichever number is directly across from 16 f.p.s. will be the correct diaphragm setting. In the meter shown, the correct reading was 11.

4   If you are filming under artificial light, use the correct light bulbs to match the type of film in your camera. For example, 16 mm Ektachrome Commercial film uses 250-watt light bulbs of 3200 K. Kodachrome II uses No. 1 photoflood bulbs.

light meter

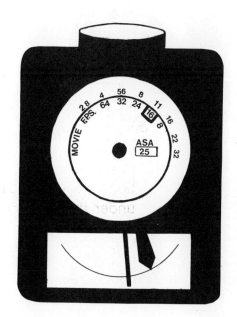

47

Positioning Art

The camera on the tripod points down at the artwork on the table. The background of the art should be fastened securely to the table-top so that it cannot shift position during filming. Look through the viewfinder of the camera to be sure that the art is centered and fills the whole screen. Most cameras will take a little more than you see through the viewfinder, especially at a distance of about 18 inches from the artwork.

You should allow for this when positioning the camera. Usually the extra is about three-quarters of an inch on all sides. To avoid taking a picture of the table as well as the art, move the camera in slightly to get a smaller picture. As mentioned before, cover the tabletop under the artwork with some sort of black material, so that if the picture does overlap it will not be as noticeable when run through the projector.

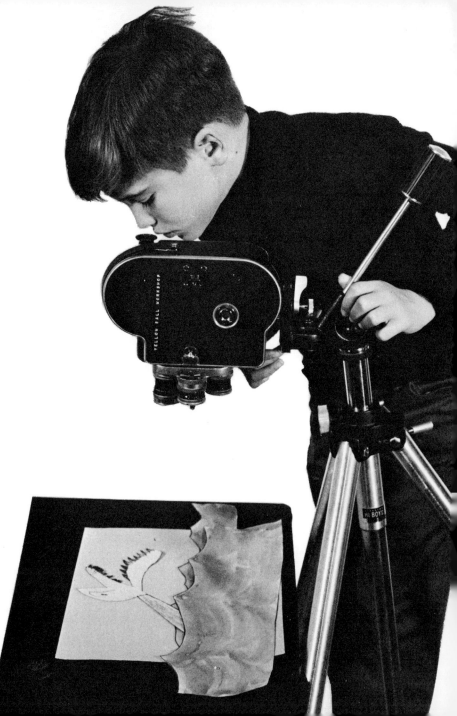

Focusing

If your camera has reflex focusing, turn the distance ring until the picture appears sharp and clear through the viewfinder. If the camera will not focus closer than 4 feet, attach a close-up lens, or follow the instructions for focusing given on the previous pages.

Lighting

If you are using artificial light, position your light stands on either side of the table. They should point down at the artwork at a 45-degree angle. Be sure you have the right kind of bulbs in the camera to match the film you are using. All other lights should be turned off. Take a light reading, and set your lens diaphragm.

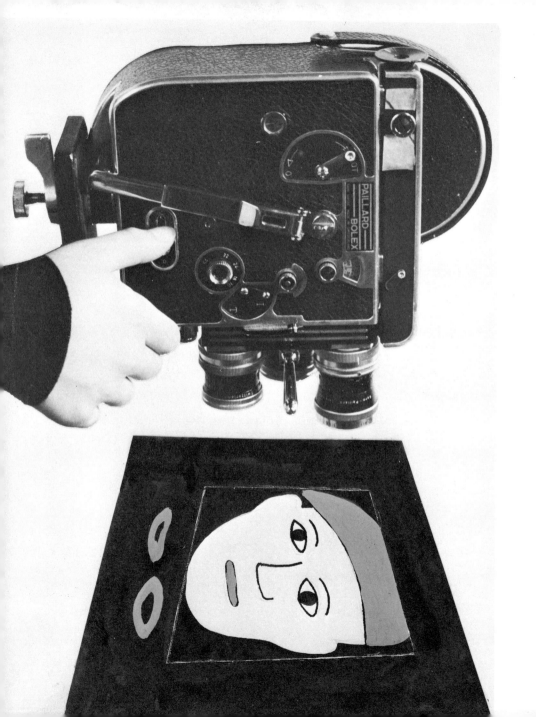

ANIMATION

Now your camera is all set up. You are ready to film your first scene. Place the small mouth on the face. Press the single-frame button of the camera 24 times. You have just taken 24 separate still pictures. When this is run through a movie projector, it will last for one second.

Now remove the small mouth and replace it with the medium-sized mouth. Take 2 frames. Take off the medium mouth and put on the large mouth. Take 2 more frames.

Take off the large mouth and put on the medium mouth. Take 2 frames. Then take off the medium mouth and put on the small mouth. Take 24 frames.

50

The 24 frames at the beginning and end of the scene will last for one second each. This will give the audience time enough to see the scene both before and after the action part. When this scene is run through a projector, the character will open his mouth and close it very quickly . . . just long enough to say "Hi!"

If you want him to speak several words or a sentence, he should open and close his mouth about six or more times. It is not necessary to decide what he is going to say at this time. If he moves his mouth enough, later when the sound track is made you will be able to speak any sentence for him and it will seem to fit. The pictures on the right show mouth animation from side view and front view.

51

24 FRAMES

2 FRAMES

2 FRAMES

2 FRAMES

24 FRAMES

The Walk

The walk is filmed in a series of six stages.

1   Figure stands with feet together.

2   Entire figure is slid forward one-quarter inch. Left foot comes up.

3   Entire figure is slid forward one-quarter inch. Left foot comes up more.

4   Entire figure is slid forward one-quarter inch. Left foot is planted on the ground with all the body weight on it. Right foot is behind and slightly up.

5   Entire figure is slid forward slightly. Right foot closes toward left foot.

6   Whole figure is slid forward slightly. Right foot closes together with left foot.

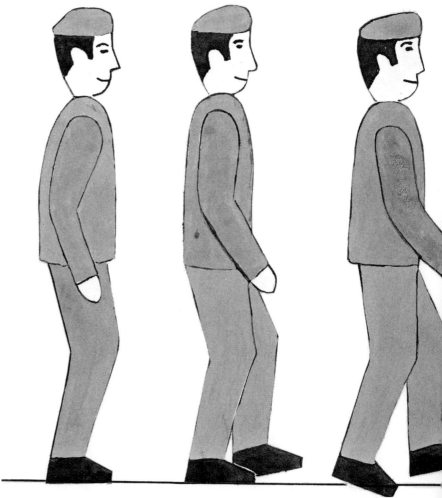

feet together   left foot up   left foot up mo

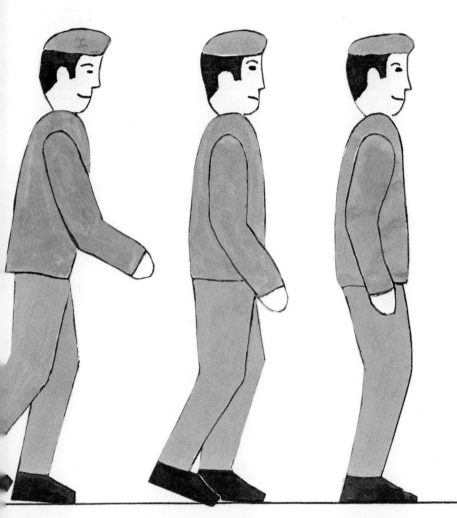

foot down   right foot closes   feet together

This action makes one step. Now repeat the action starting with the right foot. The figure is moved slightly forward each time to simulate the constant forward movement of the body as steps are being made. Each time the character is moved, two frames are taken.

The arms move in opposite action to the legs. If the right leg is forward, the left arm is forward. It is not always necessary to make both arms appear to move in unison with the legs. In fact, it is better for your first walk to move only the legs, so that you can concentrate on them. If the character is to run, he will take bigger steps and be moved forward more of a distance each time.

Turn-Around

The soldier tramps through the forest. He reaches the castle, turns, and enters a doorway. For this shot, walk him along, using the side-view figure. As his body gets exactly centered in the doorway, remove the side figure and replace it with the back figure. Film this for a few frames, and then edge him to the right with his figure sliding into the slit around the door, until he has disappeared. He leaves the building the same way, using the front figure. Only four views of the figure are needed for this operation.

54

side position: walks to entra

back view: walks behind wal

front position: moves out mo

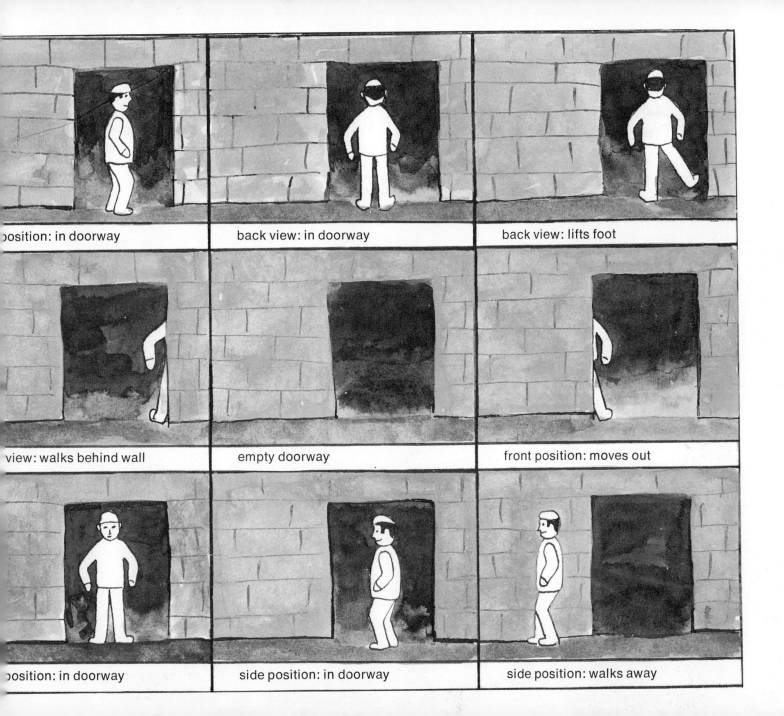

position: in doorway

back view: in doorway

back view: lifts foot

view: walks behind wall

empty doorway

front position: moves out

position: in doorway

side position: in doorway

side position: walks away

PROJECTION

Basically, a sound projector is a machine which pulls film through itself at the rate of 24 f.p.s. The film has perforations (little square holes) on each side. A claw in the projector grabs the film by these holes and pulls it forward jerkily. The film passes across a rectangular window. There is a light behind the window which shines through the film and projects the picture through the lens onto the screen. The projector shows one frame and then an instant later the shutter covers the picture while the claw pulls another frame into position in front of the window. Then the shutter opens again to shine light through the second frame.

All of this happens so fast that the eye doesn't notice that it is seeing a series of still pictures one after another at the rate of 24 per second. Since each picture is just a little different from the one before it, there is an illusion of movement. Both animated and live action movies are just a series of still pictures shown in rapid sequence.

All projectors work in this same way, but they may vary in their loading. You will just have to follow the loading directions for your particular machine. Some projectors are self-loading. With these, it is important to make sure that the head (front end) of the film is cut neatly across before you begin to feed it in.

EDITING

Editing is one of the most important steps in filmmaking. It can, and usually does, make the difference between an exciting film and a dull one. You should have good editing equipment. This includes a viewer for looking at the film, rewinds for holding the reel of film and cranking it through the viewer, and a splicer for joining together pieces of film. An editing set is like a small projector, except that the film is wound through it by hand. You can stop it to look closely at a single frame and go backward and forward with ease.

Bad scenes can be removed by simply cutting them out with scissors. The loose ends can then be glued together with a splicer. Scenes can also be rearranged. A scene filmed late in the action can be moved up to the beginning. A scene which is too long can be shortened. A long scene can be cut in half and part of it used at the beginning of the film, and the rest at a later time.

A film is a series of scenes involving close-up shots, long shots, medium shots, titles and pans. A film makes a large part of its impact from the way it is put together. You could even make several different movies using the same shots, just by putting the scenes in a different order.

In editing your film, you should keep your audience in mind. You do not want to tire them. It is a good rule never to have unnecessary scenes in your films.

The scenes in most films are shot out of sequence. The editor then puts the scenes in the proper order. The reel of film is usually placed on the left rewind and fed through the viewer onto the empty take-up reel on your right-hand side. The beginning of a scene is called its head. The end is its tail. As you cut apart the scenes, the head is taped to your work table and labeled. The tail is dropped into a clean paper bag. Never let your film drop on the floor. Dust on the films causes scratches. Your work area should be clean and free from dust.

When you are ready to put your film together, tape about 6 feet of black leader onto the right-hand reel. This amount of leader is necessary for loading the film into the projector. Then splice the head of your first scene onto the tail of the leader. Splice the head of the second scene onto the tail of the first scene, and so on. As film is added, wind it up onto the right-hand reel. When all the scenes have been spliced, add 6 feet of black leader onto the tail. Now wind the entire film backward onto the left rewind. You may now take it off and load it onto the projector for viewing.

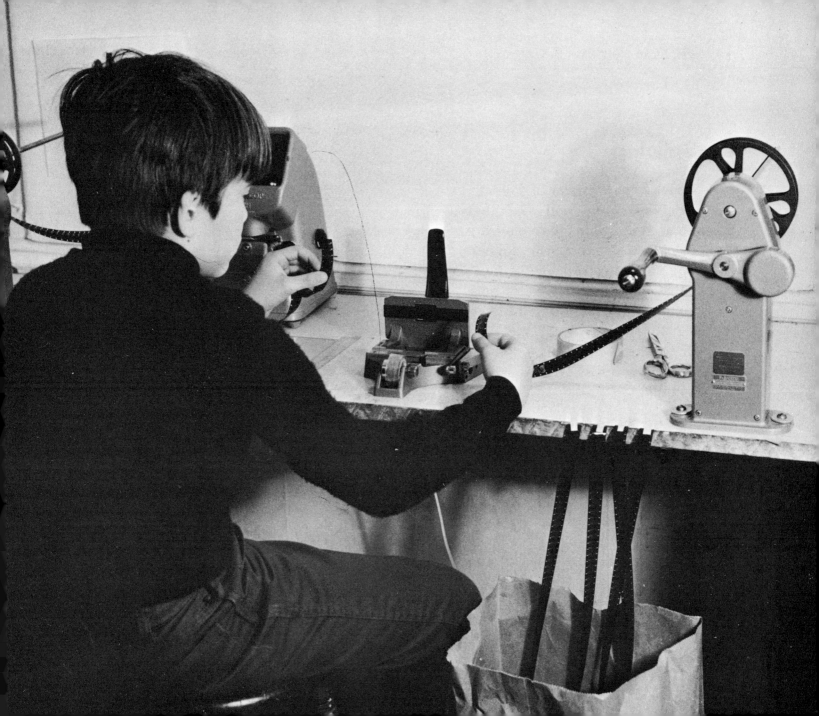

Splicing

There are two ways of splicing. One uses glue and the other tape. We prefer glue if you are using an inexpensive splicer. The splicer shown here is inexpensive and works well for both tape and glue. It may be used for 16 mm film or 8 mm and Super-8 mm films. The demonstration here is with glue and 16 mm film.

1 This splicer has two blades on each side, clamps on the bottom to hold them down and a scraper. First, lift the top right and left blades. Place the film on the right lower blade. It is held in place by the metal pins which stick up through the perforations (square holes) in the sides of the film.

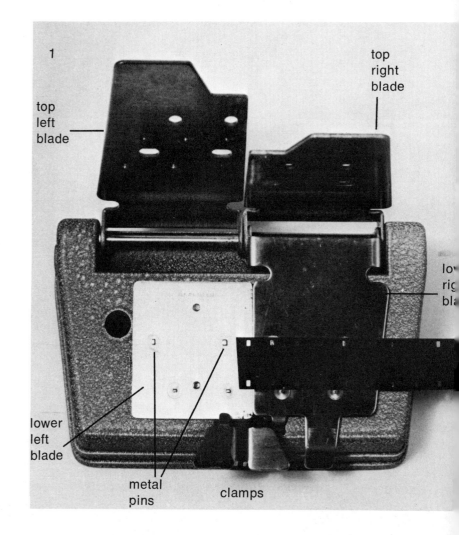

1

top left blade

top right blade

lower right blade

lower left blade

metal pins

clamps

2 The top right blade is brought down to clamp the film between the two right-hand blades. Then the two blades with the film between them are raised. The left-hand film is locked onto the pins of the left lower blade and the top left blade is brought down to hold it.

3 The two right blades are then brought down, cutting both the right and left films.

4 The two right blades are raised. The scraper is lifted partly out and rubbed across the exposed left side of the film to remove the emulsion (colored coating). It is easier to scrape this coating off if you wet it slightly with water first. A film has two sides. The dull side of the film with the picture on it is the emulsion. The other side is shiny and is the acetate base.

scraper

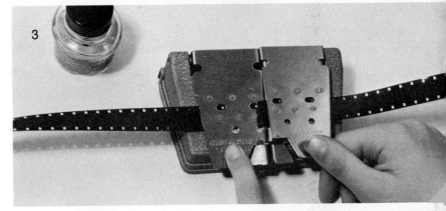

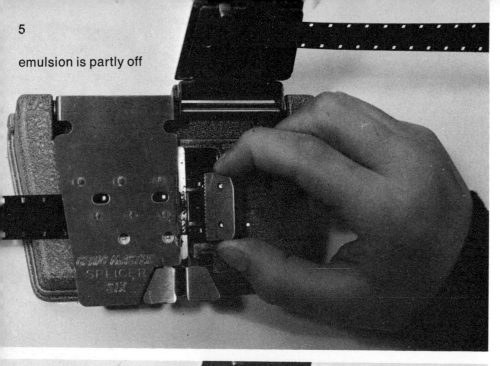

5

emulsion is partly off

5   In this picture you can see that all of the emulsion is not off. The film must be scraped until it is perfectly clear. Be careful not to tear the film. For your first few splices, it would be a good idea to practice on black leader or scrap film, rather than your valuable scenes.

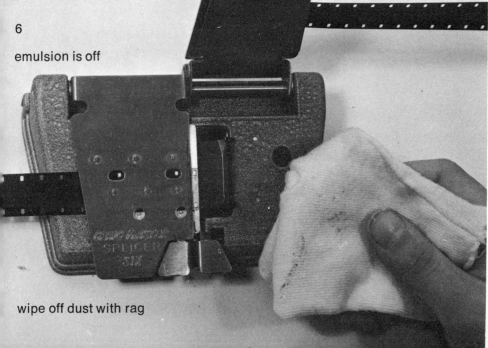

6

emulsion is off

wipe off dust with rag

6   A clean rag is used to wipe all the dust from the splicing area. The area must be clean and dry before the splicing glue is applied.

7 Here a small dab of splicing liquid is applied to the splice area and then the blades, with the film sandwiched in between, are brought down quickly and tightly. Be sure to screw the top back on the splicing liquid. It will evaporate and lose strength if it is left open.

apply dab of splicing glue

8 Let the film set for about twenty seconds. Then carefully lift the top right and left blades, and peel the film out. If it is a good splice, it will run smoothly through a projector and will hardly be visible. If it is a poor splice, take it apart and make the whole thing again. A poor splice will cause the film to tear in the projector.

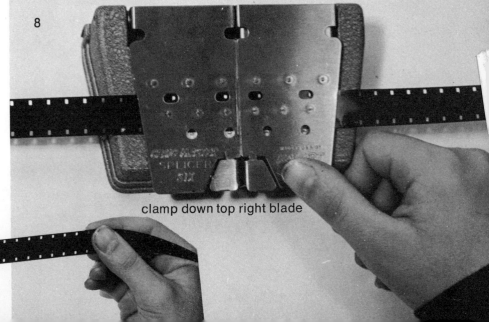

8

clamp down top right blade

SOUND

When you show your films, you may want to have sound effects. The simplest way is to play a record or tape along with the picture. If you want to have special effects or voices, you can make these on a tape recorder. Many types of sounds can be made using the human voice alone. Other sounds are easier if you have some tools, such as horns, cellophane, Chinese gongs, or wind-bells, slide whistles, straws and cans of water. Some sounds can be bought ready-made on tapes or records. Sounds already recorded can be changed by recording them again at a slower or faster speed.

Fire	Crinkle cellophane.
Explosions	Make with mouth close to microphone.
Rain	Pour uncooked rice into metal can.
Fog	Use a horn or blow through a metal pipe.
Birds	Use a bird whistle or your voice.
Horse galloping	Slap your hands against your knees.
Gunshot	Clap sticks together or shoot a cap pistol.
Automobile	Use your voice.

Synchronizing Sound with Picture

The most efficient way to make a sound tape which is synchronized with the picture is to run the projector and record the sounds at the same time. To do this, you must have the machine in another room, projecting the picture through a glass window onto a screen in the sound recording room. The reason for this is that the projector makes a noise when it is running. The tape recorder will record this noise if the projector is in the same room.

Another way of making a sound tape is to record the sound effects by themselves and then edit them to fit the picture. In *The Mailman and the Dog,* the first sound is a whistle. Record someone whistling for a while. Attach some white leader to your tape just in front of the whistling sound.

1　Load the film into the projector.
2　Load the sound tape into the tape recorder.
3　The first sound should be directly opposite the sound head.
4　Give the tape recorder time to warm up.
5　Turn on the projector. At first you should see only leader. As soon as you see the first picture appear, release the tape recorder so that sound and picture run together.
6　The instant the scene for the whistle ends, turn off the tape recorder.
7　Any whistling sound you have left over will be extra. Cut this off and throw it away. Now you know that you have enough whistle sound.
8　The dog growl is spliced onto the end of the whistle sound.
9　Rewind the film in the projector until it is at the beginning of the film. Rewind the tape in the projector until the first whistle sound is directly in front of the head.
10　Run both sound and picture through again until the growl scene is finished. Stop the tape recorder and cut off all excess growl sound.
11　Continue adding all your sounds until the film is finished.

Splicing Sound Tape

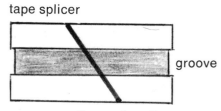

tape splicer

groove

diagonal cut line

flick off leftover
white leader

tape

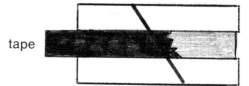

press sound tape in
groove to overlap
diagonal cut line

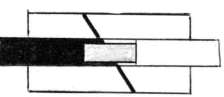

press splicing tape across
diagonal cut line and onto
the sound tape and leader

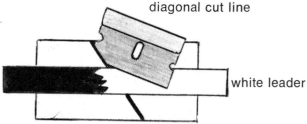

white leader

press white leader or other
sound tape into right-hand
groove to overlap diagonal cut;

fit single-edge razor blade into
diagonal slit and cut across
white leader and tape

peel out finished
spliced tape

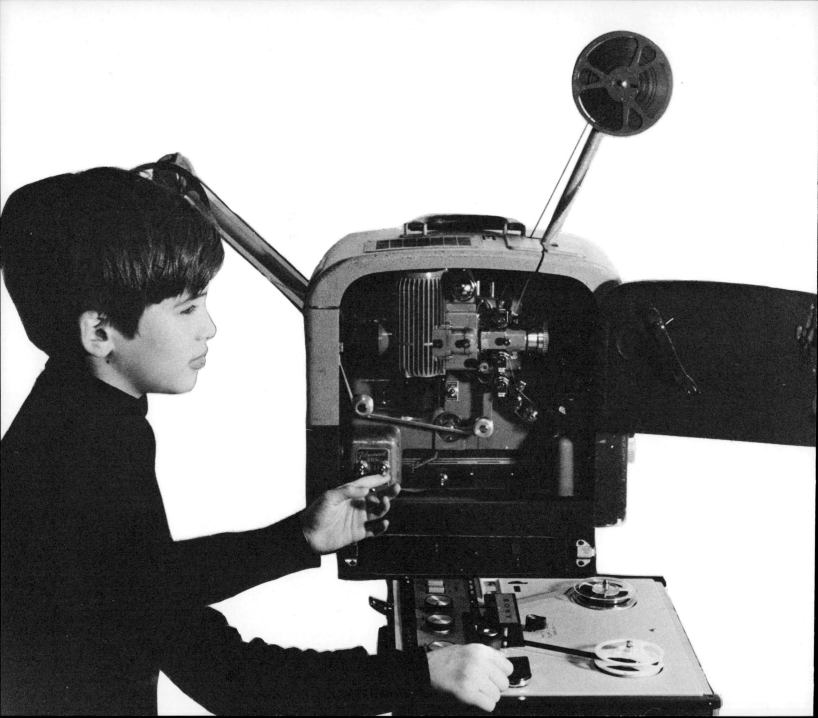

You now have a tape recording which has perfectly synchronized sound effects. Each time you show the movie, your sound effects will occur at the right time, *if:*

1   You always use the same projector and tape recorder. Different machines will run at slightly different speeds. Using someone else's equipment will cause your synchronization (synch) to be off.

2   You use the right recording tape. Some tapes stretch. We like Scotch tape No. 111 which has an acetate base.

The best way of keeping your sound and picture together is to have sound and picture put on the same film by a lab. In Super-8 mm film, your film can have a magnetic sound stripe added along one side, and the sound recorded to synchronize. To play this back, you must have the proper kind of projector. Another technique is to have a projector and tape recorder run in synch together, using a special attachment.

If the film is 16 mm, you can have a film lab make a professional, optical sound print of your film. This is a copy which has both picture and optical sound together on one film. To do this, you must give the lab both the film and the quarter-inch sound tape, together with a sound sheet which tells them where the most important effects will occur.

flip the cards
through your hands
to see the movement

FLIP CARDS

Flip card films have a quivery, alive look that is not found in other types of animation. A simple drawing is made upon a small card about 4″ x 6″. On each successive card, the drawing is slightly altered. When the cards are flipped through the fingers, the drawing seems to move. This way you can check the action before you film the cards.

You should keep flip card drawings simple, since you will have to draw them over and over. The art materials for this are simple too. Most of the time we use the small white 4″ x 6″ scratch pads which can be bought in any stationery store. Thin felt-tip pens are used for drawing. The paper is thin enough to see through. Make the first drawing. Then lay the second piece of paper on top and repeat the drawing, changing just the part which has to move. The boy waving his arm is drawn exactly the same over and over again, except for the arm, which is drawn in different positions.

The three types of movement are especially suited to flip cards:
1 Movement across a page (boy saluting)
2 Movement toward the camera (whale swimming)
3 Back and forth movement (dancers)

Flip cards are placed under the camera and each one is filmed for 2 frames. This will give smooth action. If you do not want to make so many drawings, you can film each one for 4 frames. This will double the length of time each scene lasts. If you film each one for 8 frames, the action will move forward in a jerky way with a kind of beat. This is effective for some films.

If you have a scene which you want to hold in one position for a while, a title for example, you should draw two versions and alternate them under the camera. They should be filmed for about 24 frames for each word in the title. This will give the audience time to read. If you made just one title drawing and filmed it for 24 frames, the quivery motion would stop, and your film would seem to stand still. In the dance scene shown on the previous page, four drawings were made. The four drawings were filmed in alternation back and forth many times. This technique saves time and energy.

White index cards can also be used. These flip through the fingers better, since they are stiff, but you cannot see through them. If you keep your art simple and bold, this doesn't matter. The reason for the delightful quivery look of films made with flip cards is that each successive drawing very seldom matches perfectly the one before it.

Flip cards are very small. The camera must be positioned close to the artwork, so that the picture will fill the entire screen. It is usually necessary to put a close-up lens over your regular lens when filming these small cards. Again, it is also wise to film on top of a black background, in case the camera takes a little more than you expected.

CLAY

Krazy Times is a clay animated film. The characters and sets are all made of clay. A clay bus roars up to the entrance of a zoo. Dozens of little clay people jump out. The bus driver sighs, wipes his forehead, and melts onto the ground in a puddle. A crazy little clay man, feeding ducks in a pond, falls in. The zoo keeper has to pull him out. The man watches some birds and imitates their actions with his arms. His arms turn into wings. A group of clay people laugh at the birds. A zoo dog is insulted by the noisy staring people. He pouts, "This zoo rots! I hate this zoo!"

The little man leaves the zoo followed by a herd of elephants, large and small. The furious zoo keeper runs out of the gate screaming for them to come back. Two large birds sitting on the gate fly into the air, releasing bird droppings all over the zoo keeper.

Krazy Times was made by a group of children varying in age from eight to thirteen. Each child made one of the characters and one of the sets. The sets were: the hill over which the bus drove, the entrance to the zoo, the pond with bridge and ducks, the street with bench, various park scenes with flowers and trees, statues, animal enclosures, and the exit for the zoo.

The film was photographed in black and white. The ground area of the sets was clay, the sky area was kept dark and shadowy so that the characters would show up. This was done by having a painted black background in the back which was kept out of focus. In three-dimensional animation, the sets are deep. You usually cannot keep the whole area in sharp focus when you are working at close quarters. Therefore you should have the middle depth of the scene — the area where the important action will take place — in sharp focus. It makes a very nice effect if some of the background is a little blurred, so long as the main character is sharp.

All the scenes were filmed with the camera pointed in a horizontal position, except for the birds flying in the air. For this scene, birds were laid down on a painted sky, and the camera was pointed down at them as for cutout animation. The characters were kept simple and not too detailed. They took on their personality by the way they moved. It would be very hard, for instance, to have a fancy character in pin-striped trousers. Every time you handled him to make him take a step, his pin stripes would be smeared out.

The characters can be made to walk in the same way as cutouts. They can walk across the scene or toward or away from the camera. In clay animation, you should take advantage of the basic ability of clay to change shape. Your man can grow taller or shorter; he is a plastic man. His arms or legs can stretch out suddenly to enormous lengths. He can melt or grow larger. He can completely change character and go from man to beast.

Your camera should be placed to film the action from different angles. Be sure to have plenty of close-up shots. Clay has a nice mushy appearance on film. Take advantage of the fingerprints and the other indentations in the clay. Lighting is very important in clay animation, as you are working with clay of one color most of the time. You will be using light and dark areas to show the action instead of flat colors. Most of the time we move the characters every 4 frames in clay animation, to cut down on the work.

DRAWING ON FILM

It is possible to make a movie without a camera. This is done by drawing directly on film. Clear leader, white leader, and black leader is purchased on 100-foot reels. Spread some white paper on your work table. Tape down about three or four feet of leader to work on at one time. The rest may be left on the reel and unwound as you need it.

The clear and white leader can be drawn on with felt-tip pens and special colored inks called Pelican-T for Plastic Sheets. They may be purchased in art supply stores. Pelican black india ink may also be used. The inks are applied with small watercolor brushes or pen points on pen holders. Any felt-tip pen that will draw on acetate is usable. One side of the leader will take the inks better than the other. Check this by sketching lightly on both sides.

82

Black leader is clear leader with a black coating. If the coating (emulsion) is scratched off, the scratched portion will be white when it is projected on a movie screen. Any sharp object may be used to scratch designs into the leader. The best scratcher we have is a line cutter for silk screen stencils. A single-edged razor blade may also be used. After a design is scratched onto the leader, it may be filled in with color. This will give you a colored design on a black background. Your first drawing on film should be a decorative experiment. Think of the strip of film as a long piece of paper to decorate. When this work dries (five minutes for felt markers, fifteen minutes for inks) you can load it in a projector and screen it. The effect will be somewhat like an abstract light show. The advantage of drawing on film is that you can see the results immediately. You don't have to wait to have the film developed.

After you have worked in this way with film, you may want to try special effects or drawing on one frame at a time. Remember that for one second of movie time, you must draw 24 frames. One frame of film is the space between the perforations. If you have a design like an explosion, a flower, a face, or a word, you must draw it at least twelve times to have it last long enough to be seen by the audience. If you use words, three-letter words are easy. You will probably make short films about three to seven feet long using this technique. If you take the two ends of your finished film and splice them together, you will then have a film loop. This loop can be loaded into the projector and run continuously. This will enable you to see the film over and over without rethreading the projector.

FILM LOOP
THREADED
ON PROJECTOR

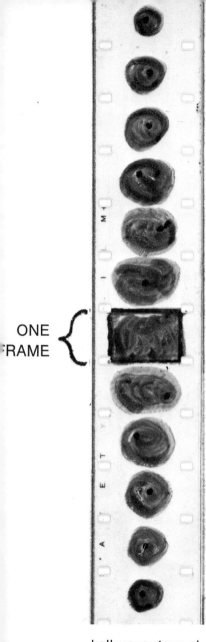

ONE FRAME

ball moves toward
camera and away

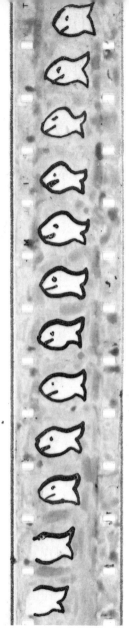

fish swims by

boat sails

car drives
over a hill

abstract design
on clear leader

face smiles

scratched design
on black leader

the word GO

TEAROUTS

Tearouts are a very good technique to use if you have no ideas for a story. You will need a package of construction paper, rubber cement, thread and tape. First you tear large shapes out of construction paper. Then tear out smaller shapes of other colors and allow these smaller shapes to fall upon the first shapes. Rearrange these shapes on top of the larger shapes until a face appears. Strange and interesting characters can be developed this way. The colored paper floats through the air and the character almost creates himself. Once the face is developed, it will give you ideas for the body and a background.

The barroom scene on the right, from *Black Hat,* was developed this way. Three students made the characters separately. They turned out to be two cowboys and a marshal. In this scene, one of the characters pours himself a drink, sips it, burps, and asks, "Hey, Sheriff, how come you're not in your office today?" The sheriff sips his Coke and bellows, "This is my office!" The other cowboy asks, "What would you do if there was a robbery in town?" The sheriff answers, "There's not going to be a robbery in this town. Anyway, I'd be able to take care of it!" The bartender asks, "Anybody want a drink, any-o-youse?" Then the saloon door bursts open and a character screams, "Sheriff, the bank's been robbed, and the bandit got away!" The animation in this scene was done the same way as for cutouts, except for the pink straw. This was gradually painted brown to look as if the Coke was being sucked up the straw.

PIXILLATION

Pixillation is a technique using live actors. In normal live action filming, the cameraman presses the exposure release button to make the camera run continuously. The camera takes the usual 24 f.p.s. An actor, moving in front of the camera will have 24 still photos taken of him every second the camera is running. When this is run through a projector at the rate of 24 f.p.s., the action will seem very smooth.

In pixillation, the cameraman presses the single-frame button twice, then the actor can change his position, or the scene or props can be changed in some way before the cameraman resumes filming. It is very similar to regular animation. The actor is like an animated figure. Because the cameraman has such control of the action, all sorts of magic things can happen.

In the pixillated film *Fat Feet,* the main character is a policeman. He is standing in a street directing traffic. Suddenly, his arms get long. This "long arm of the law" is made by using a fake hand and arm. The fake hand and arm are mounted on a stick, which is tucked into the sleeve of the policeman's coat. The camera takes 2 frames and stops. An assistant runs into the scene and moves the arm a little. The assistant gets out of the

range of the camera. The camera takes 2 more frames. The assistant runs back into the scene to move the fake arm out again. Then the camera takes 2 frames, and so on, until the arm is stretched out full length. In this scene the cars which drive by are three-quarters life size. They are cut from large sheets of heavy cardboard and are braced on the back with thin strips of wood. The persons who drive them are real. The drivers sit on small stools behind the cars. Every 2 frames, the driver moves the car forward about 4 inches. An assistant runs out to turn the hub caps of the wheels to give the illusion of rolling wheels.

Pixillated films have a fast-moving, abrupt type of action. Our students have made many interesting pixillated films using masks and costumes. The mask in *Baby Face Gordon* was a paper bag painted with poster paint. The hair was fake Halloween hair bought at a dime store. The costume was brown wrapping paper, folded over, with a hole cut for the head to go through. The sides of the bag were stapled together. The costume was painted. The arms of the live actor inside the costume were covered with a sweater of the same color as the top part of the costume. For example, if a character was wearing a black coat, as in *Baby Face Gordon,* a black sweater was worn to cover the arms. The bag part of the costume was made long, and we avoided filming the feet. Cheap white work gloves from a hardware store covered the hands. These gloves look like the gloves some animated characters wear. We found that it was best to cover the entire body in costume in order to maintain the illusion of a magic character.

costume is wrapping paper folded over and stapled together at the sides

paper bag head

white work gloves

Instead of filming live action, the cameraman pressed the single-frame button over and over. In between clicks, the assistant ran in to help pull the money out of the bank teller's window.

The students painted large backdrops for their characters to perform against, using large rolls of heavy brown wrapping paper. Pieces of this paper 36 inches wide and 7 feet long were hung against the wall from ceiling to floor. Then they were painted with poster paint.

In *Baby Face Gordon,* the background was painted white, with a bank teller's window. The bank teller was painted in so that he could be an animated figure. Other scenes we have done are a Harlem street with a subway entrance, a barroom, a fashion model's studio, a hippie hangout, a desolate swamp-desert scene, and a black sky with white stars for Santa Claus to fly through on his sled.

In some scenes the props are very important. In the film *Santa,* a live actor in a costume seems to fly through the air in a modern motorized sled. The sled body was a large cardboard box painted red and outfitted with two flashing red lights in front. The runners for the sled were made of cardboard, covered with a plaster material used for making plaster casts for broken arms and legs. This is called Paris craft. The sled was placed on top of a strong metal tea table and the actor climbed up into it. The tea table was covered with black paper to match the sky background. An assistant pushed the tea table a little, and the cameraman started filming. All the while, Santa was waving his arms, and an assistant was turning the red lights off and on. It is a beautiful and fantastic scene.

FILM EQUIPMENT

CAMERA   Your movie camera can be either 8 mm, Super-8 mm or 16 mm. It is preferable if your camera has a single-frame release, and reflex viewing and reflex focusing.

TRIPOD   A tripod or tilting stand is necessary to hold the camera steady.

EDITING SET   Editing is done with a viewer, splicer, and rewinds. Sometimes these are all combined in one set.

LIGHT METER   This is necessary if your movie camera does not have a built-in electric-eye exposure control.

LIGHT STANDS   You won't need these if your filming is done during the daytime, next to a window.

PROJECTOR   This is used for showing your films.

MOVIE SCREEN   The finished film is projected onto a movie screen or a white wall, or on a large sheet of white cardboard.

ART SUPPLIES

CUTOUTS For cutout animation, you will need scissors, tape, thread, paper (or thin cardboard) and either crayons, felt-tip markers, or poster paint and brushes.

CLAY For clay animation, use soft, nonhardening plastilina.

TEAROUTS For tearout animation, use construction paper of assorted colors, tape and thread.

FLIP CARDS For flip card animation, use white scratch pads with sheets 4" x 6", and thin-tipped felt pens.

DRAWING ON FILM For drawing directly on film, use clear 16 mm film leader and felt-tip marking pens.

PIXILLATED FILMS Pixillated films use real, live actors, sometimes in paper costumes and masks. For this, you can use paper bags and rolls of wrapping paper or crepe paper. These are colored with poster paint and crayons.

FILMOGRAPHY

Al Kaseltzer Strikes Again by four students aged eleven to sixteen. Art by Amy Kravitz, eleven. Newton Creative Arts Center, 1966.

The Amazing Colossal Man, a group project created by students aged five to twelve at the Yellow Ball Workshop, 1964. Story by Steve DeTore, twelve. Creature by Arthur DeTore, ten.

Atomic Robot by Paul Falcone, eight. Cellar Door Cinema, 1967.

Baby Face Gordon by Clifford Ginandes, thirteen, and Patrick Quinlan, fourteen. This scene by Clifford Ginandes. Cellar Door Cinema, 1968.

Black Hat by a group of students, aged eight to thirteen. Art by Paul Falcone, Geoffery Lenk, and Donald Stendahl. Cellar Door Cinema, 1967.

Charley and His Harley by Mark Mahoney, twelve. Newton Creative Arts Center, 1969.

Cinder City by Michael Schmertzler, thirteen, Christopher Lenk, fourteen, and Peter Bull, eleven. Art by Michael Schmertzler. Cellar Door Cinema, 1966.

Fat Feet, directed by Red Grooms, photographed by Yvonne Andersen, starring Dominic Falcone and Mimi Gross. Produced by Dominic Falcone and Red Grooms. A Yellow Ball-Ruckus Film, 1966.

$50,000 per Fang by Steve DeTore, thirteen, assisted by Arthur DeTore, eleven, and Michael DeGregorio, fourteen. Art by Steve DeTore and Arthur DeTore. Yellow Ball Workshop, 1965.

Just a Fishment of My Imagination by Carol Sones, seventeen. Newton Creative Arts Center, 1969.

In the Middle by Karen Warschaurer, eleven. Newton Creative Arts Center, 1966.

Krazy Times by a group of students aged eight to thirteen. Character by Paul Falcone, eight, set by Sherry Domigan, thirteen. Cellar Door Cinema, 1967.

The Mailman and the Dog, by Janet Yates, nine, and Rita Fantasia, ten. Yellow Ball Workshop, 1965.

Punky's Delema by Carol Sones, sixteen. Newton Creative Arts Center, 1968.

Santa by Robert Reiffan, ten. Cellar Door Cinema, 1968.

Spectator by Steffen Pierce, fourteen. Cellar Door Cinema, 1967.

Stanley the Pink Unicorn by Amy Kravitz, twelve. Newton Creative Arts Center, 1968.

Sylvia I by Amy Schmertzler, twelve, and Tod Feinberg, eleven. Cellar Door Cinema, 1967.

Three Blind Mice by Timothy Hegarty, seven. Yellow Ball Workshop, 1965.

Trip to the Unknown by Sean O'Leary, twelve, and Steve Lanes, thirteen. Newton Creative Arts Center, 1969.

Underwater Creatures by Paul Falcone, six, assisted by Jean Falcone, four, and Billy Gibbs, seven. Art by Paul Falcone. Yellow Ball Workshop, 1965.

Yellow Submarine by Elsa Glassman, sixteen. Cellar Door Cinema, 1967.

Students pictured:
Jean Falcone
Paul Falcone
Billy Fuchs
Amy Kravitz and Mimi Kravitz
Lianne McKayle
Mark Winer

Book text and design by Yvonne Andersen
Photographs by Yvonne Andersen, Dominic Falcone, Joanne
  Ricca
Line drawings by Paul Falcone, Jean Falcone, Yvonne Andersen

INDEX

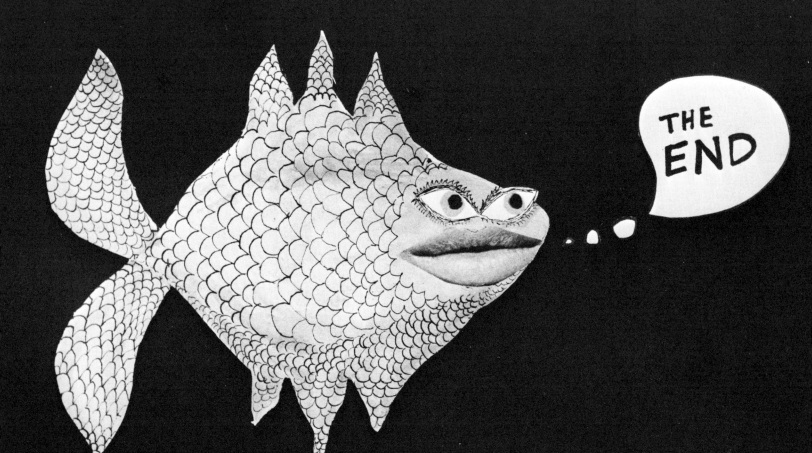